# MILFORD HAVEN

## MORE THAN AN OIL PORT

by

Derek E Davies and Desmond G Davies

# FOREWORD

The title of the book says it all, of course - for 50 years Milford Haven has built its reputation and expanded its activities on the basis of its support for the oil industry, which was the catalyst for the Authority to be created as the Conservancy Board through the Act of 1958.

Business expansion and growth over the intervening years have, however, allowed us to move into other areas which insofar as they relate to handling different types of shipping to oil tankers are aptly demonstrated in this excellent publication.

Also, whilst 50 years is a fair chunk of history of which we can be proud some of the developments that we have undertaken have enabled us to adopt an even wider historical perspective. Thus, the purchase of the Milford Docks Company in 1989 takes us back to 1874 when the Milford Docks Company was established with the intention of accommodating ocean liners which, whilst they did not materialise, did in the guise of "Sybil", the first vessel to enter the Docks, firmly establish the importance of fishing to the port's activities. However, that original ambition for transatlantic liners has been translated into the more modem equivalent of the cruise ships which are starting to become regular visitors to the Port - again, as can be seen within these pages.

In summary, I hope all readers will agree that what the authors and photographers have outlined for us all here is an apt demonstration of the way in which Milford Haven Port Authority is successfully moving to achieve our vision of becoming the most highly regarded port in the UK.

**Ted Sangster,**
Chief Executive, Milford Haven Port Authority

**Milford Haven Port Authority**

Copyright © 2007 by Desmond and Derek Davies. The right of Desmond and Derek Davies to be identified as authors of this work has been asserted by them in accordance with the Copyright, Design and Patent Act 1998.

Published by Bernard McCall, "Halia", 400 Nore Road, Portishead, Bristol, BS20 8EZ
Website: www.coastalshipping.co.uk
Telephone/fax: 01275 846178. E-mail: bernard@coastalshipping.co.uk
All distribution enquiries should be addressed to the publisher.

Printed by Cromwell Press, Aintree Avenue, White Horse Business Park, Trowbridge, Wiltshire, BA14 0XB
Telephone : 01225 711400. Fax : 01225 711249
E-mail : books@cromwellpress.co.uk
Website : www.cromwellpress.co.uk
Cover images: Roger Paice & Mark Richards www.photowales.com

ISBN : 978-1-902953-31-1

# C O N T E N T S

# INTRODUCTION
## <u>Milford Haven - More Than An Oil Port</u>

Over the years, the small ports around the Milford Haven waterway have fulfilled a number of maritime roles. One or other has been at some time in its existence a ferry port, a whaling port, a fishing port, a shipbuilding town, and, between the years 1939 to 1945, the waterway itself became a convoy assembly port. But it was not until the arrival of the oil industry in the Haven in 1960 that the emphasis moved away from the fortunes of the small and frankly not very successful towns around the Haven to a waterway dominated by the activities of the oil industry. Oil refineries were built for Esso, Amoco, Gulf and Texaco. An import terminal was built to serve BP's refinery at Llandarcy, near Swansea.

The oil industry and its five terminals brought with it the need to think bigger than the parish pump politics of small towns. The need for rule and order over the entire waterway which the ever-increasing size of ships demanded required the establishment of a controlling authority and, though the Milford Haven Port Authority preceded the arrival of the oil industry, the industry's arrival ensured the Authority's continued existence and development.

The oil industry was instrumental in the growth of a variety of small, and some not-so-small industries around the Haven and they in turn have created their own specific demands on the Haven. The revenues arising from the oil trade and the need to update and improve facilities, have meant that in essence the Milford Haven Port Authority has become a Marine Economic Development Agency.

On today's waterway, the oil industry still dominates the scene. In 2006 there are two active refineries, the larger Chevron refinery at Pembroke, and a smaller Total refinery at Milford Haven. These were originally the Texaco and Amoco refineries respectively. To the east of the town of Milford Haven, Semlogisitics operates a storage facility at its Waterston site, once the Gulf refinery. But in addition to that there is the marine traffic generated by the ferry terminal at Pembroke Dock with its connection to Rosslare, the fishing industry at Milford Docks out of which a small fleet of vessels of several nations operates, the Naval base at Pembroke Dock, the dry cargo activities of the Port of Pembroke, the ship repair traffic at Milford Docks, and the traffic generated by the engineering industries which have slowly developed around the Haven. And to add to this there is the slow growth of an infant cruise ship industry. In 2003, the waterway discovered that it would become the port of entry for a major portion of the UK's imported liquefied natural gas (LNG). The immediate impact of that was to bring to the waterway a host of craft from the marine construction industry and their associated cargoes. As for the LNG ships themselves, well, they are still to come.

In the year ended 31 December 2006, the port handled ships with a total tonnage of 49,445,873 gross tonnes, making it the fourth busiest port in the UK. (See Appendix I for more detail). This book is an assembly of photographs which tries to represent the 3000 plus working ships which make up that tonnage. Its purpose is twofold. Given the fact that the entire waterway is flanked by a coastal path it is almost impossible to ignore the movements on the water. Hopefully the book will help watchers to appreciate what it is that they are seeing. Secondly, it is an attempt to explain what the ships might be doing and why. Each class of ship is accorded its own section and a range of photos is included giving examples of the different members of any class. For many of the ships, this is quite simple. Fishing vessels with their fishing numbers on their sides and the tools of their trade scattered across their decks are quite easy to identify, describe and classify.

But the oil industry tankers are not such an easy task. The oil trade is international, very complex and very, very large. Though inside the oil industry, ships are categorised by size and function, to the average observer it is extremely difficult to detect and understand such operational differences. The smallest oil ships, the coasters, are easy to explain. They are and do what their names say they do. They carry oil products around the coast. But once one gets above the size of about 5,000 tonnes, trying to nail down a vessel to a trade is a pointless operation because it doesn't work that way. So we have simply shown oil tankers in increasing sizes and tried to explain some of the intricacies of the oil trade in passing. We have suggested what trade they might be involved in, where they have been built and what features point to that origin, and we have offered comments on who might own the vessels. We have tried to mix the everyday and the unusual. But in such a small book there are limits to what can be achieved.

Economic facts say that if you increase the size of a cargo, the lower the cost of moving each tonne becomes, and the greater the distance the bigger the savings. So, theoretically, bigger ships ought to travel the longer routes. Indeed, obtaining economies of scale in carrying crude oil over the long distances from the Middle East was the great goal which originally brought the oil industry to the port in the first place. So the bigger the ship, the farther it will have travelled.

If only life would be that simple. In the oil trade, the discovery of North Sea oil changed all that. The bulk of the crude oil now used by the port refineries comes from that province just around the corner. And with it came a new and distinctive breed of oil tanker, the shuttle tanker. To lift oil cargoes from production platforms out in deep water, the oil industry created a sophisticated variant of the oil tanker able to do just this and whose most obvious identifying characteristic is a large and often ungainly bow loading assembly. But the end result of this technological development is that some of the largest vessels now using the port are these giant "commuting" tankers.

The maturing of the North Sea oil province and the enduring reality that most of the world's crude oil is still miles from our shores has meant that economies of scale will still support the case for the large tanker. Thus crude oil arriving in the Haven from the Middle East or West Africa will tend to arrive in such vessels, large range and Very Large Crude Carriers - the celebrated VLCC. In oil industry parlance, a VLCC is a vessel of over 160,000 deadweight tonnes.

In the text, the terms "gross tonnage" and "deadweight tonnage" are abbreviated to gt and dwt respectively. A short note is included on page 60 for readers who are unfamiliar with ship tonnages. Where reference is made to vessel ownership, the details relate to the situation at the date of the photograph.

To make the book more relevant, and particularly so to the visitor, we have tried to show that the shipping can be observed from a whole host of places. To each photograph we have attached a "location letter" which can be linked to the map on page 62. Some of them have been accumulated literally "out through the car window". Many have involved a relatively easy stroll with a good pair of shoes. None of them would have taxed a moderately fit walker. And all of them have been taken without breaking the law of the land.

Most of the photos show blue skies and calm seas for obvious reasons. A few show less clement conditions. But readers wishing to avail themselves of the opportunity to see things for themselves would do well to remember that Milford Haven is an Atlantic coast port. The complexion of the natives comes, not out of a bottle, but by courtesy of the wind and the rain. Come suitably prepared!

Almost as a postscript and to prove that the shipping world changes rapidly, as we go to press comes news that the Total oil refinery has been acquired by Murco.

Derek E Davies and Desmond G Davies                    Steynton, November 2007

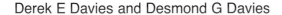

Construction work on the two new LNG terminals has brought a wide variety of vessels to the Haven. On 8 October 2006, the **Coronel** (ANT, 2089gt/78) was photographed alongside the **Boa Barge 10** at the South Hook terminal. The coaster was loading crushed concrete from the former Esso jetty which previously occupied this site.

*(Vic Smith)*

## ACKNOWLEDGEMENTS

This book lays no claims to being a scientific, nautical or economic treatise. It is a simple series of observations based on regular contact and meanderings around the waterway. The choice of ships, and the balance in that choice, is based on the daily movement sheets which the Port Authority has been good enough to make available to us over an extended period. Our principal "reference book" has been the ever-faithful Lloyd's Register of Shipping, though for those seeking more detailed information on the ports of the waterway there are several excellent texts available.

We would wish to acknowledge the help of our publisher who helped to turn an idea into reality, and we would wish to acknowledge the help of the Port Authority who, whilst not interfering in any way in what we did, supported us in the task. But if this text has to be dedicated to anyone, then it must be the ladies of the Port Authority's administrative section who religiously every day set aside for us a copy of the daily movement sheet. Those sheets provide the information on which we based the whole scheme for this small book. Rarely can the odd box of chocolates have brought such a return. The mistakes of course are and remain our responsibility.

Though the waterway, like many UK ports of today, has no home grown fleet, the two remaining waterway refineries "support" a small fleet of coastal tankers and some of these ships are effectively based in the port. From Milford Haven, they deliver refined products, principally to the west coast of the UK and to Ireland. The **Blackrock** (GBR, 1646gt/89), seen here manoeuvring to go alongside the Total refinery jetty, was a frequent visitor, in 2005 recording more than fifty calls at the port. Built in 1988 at the Selby yard of the Cochrane Shipbuilders Ltd, her original British owners, Crescent Shipping, like many other UK shipping companies, have been taken over by foreign companies, in this case by the Danish Clipper Wonsild Group.    (N)

If any company could have been said to have inherited the mantle of John Masefield's "salt caked" coasters, it was the grey-hulled fleet of F T Everard & Co, London, now part of the James Fisher Group. The waterway was and remains a principal operating port for a number of ships of this fleet. The **Arduity** (GBR, 1926gt/81), unlike most of their tankers, was acquired second hand, after a long career in the colours of Shell (UK) Ltd for whom she was launched as the **Shell Seafarer**. She was built at Goole to a design coincidentally based on a group of ships built for Everards themselves. In 1999 she and her sisterships were acquired by Everards to operate the Shell coastal shipping programme.    (B)

The **Milford Fisher** (GBR, 3368gt/98) was ordered at the Qiuxin shipyard in China under the proposed name of **Helmsman**, a name associated with the London-based firm of Rowbotham Tankers. In 1993 that firm was acquired by P&O Tankships, and then in 1996, James Fisher & Co of Barrow acquired the coastal tanker fleet of P&O. The ship was launched as **Milford Fisher** in 1997 and has been a regular caller at the port ever since. A 3,600 hp MaK engine drives this 4,975 dwt ship at a service speed of about 12 knots on her typical voyages to ports such as Galway, Limerick, Avonmouth and Belfast. (B)

An important, if unglamorous, trade emanating from most refineries will be the carriage of heavy fuel oil to provide bunker fuel for the shipping industry. The **Vingatank** (SWE, 2834gt/02) is the small coaster to which much of that trade to ports around the western UK from the waterway falls. A relatively new vessel, built for the Swedia Rederi AB of Donsö in Sweden, she is one of a growing number of small vessels operated by western European companies that have their origin in Turkish shipyards. She was built by Çelik Techne of Tuzla in Turkey and at 4,300 dwt is powered by a 2,750 hp B&W Alpha diesel engine. Amongst her routine tasks will be deliveries to the ferry ports of Fishguard and Holyhead, where, in recent years, sea borne deliveries of fuel have become the norm. (M)

Struer, on the west coast of the Jutland peninsula in Denmark, is the home of the Herning shipping fleet. This company presently operates a fleet of about a dozen small coastal tankers mainly in north-western European waters, and, of that dozen, two operate regularly out of the Haven. The **Dagmar Theresa** (DIS, 2654gt/01) is on charter to James Fisher Everard. She is one of the more modern ships in the Herning fleet, and at 4,400 dwt, also one of the largest. Like the **Vingatank**, she was built at Tuzla. The heavy foremast mounted well forward on the focsle is usually a good clue to a Turkish origin. In the photo she is seen entering the harbour on return from one of her runs to the west coast of Ireland.    (A)

Ownership has always been a complex subject in the world of ships, and the small ship sector is no exception. The **Stability** (GBR, 2630gt/04), carrying Everard funnel colours and here seen leaving Milford Docks on 22 September 2005, started life in the Istanbul yard of Gelibolu Gemi as the **Atlantis Armona**. She was originally time chartered for five years to work for Everard's. That time charter was then replaced by a bare-boat charter under which Everard's assumed responsibility for more areas of ship operation and maintenance. Thus the Everard fleet, all of whose ships sport powder grey hulls, suddenly acquired a blue-hulled ship. Later in the year, yet another would join them as the sistership, **Atlantis Aldabra,** became the **Summity** under a similar arrangement.    (C)

Vickers Shipbuilding & Engineering Ltd once built ships for some of the great shipping names of the world, though their Barrow yard is today primarily a warship building yard. In the current *Lloyd's Register*, there are three merchant ships listed as coming from that yard. The **Mersey Fisher** (GIB, 2760gt/98), and her sisterships, **Thames Fisher** and **Humber Fisher** form that list. The 4,765 dwt **Mersey Fisher** was built in 1998 for James Fisher Tankships Ltd, a company based at Barrow. With an 8-cylinder Ruston engine built at the Newton-le-Willows plant developing 3,120 hp, she is an unusual British ship - all home-made. These nicely proportioned and good looking ships are frequent users of the port.     (C)

In July 2006, the **Speciality** (GBR, 3859gt/06) arrived in the port, another new building to join the coastal tanker fleet operated by  F T Everard & Co of London. She is the third ship in the Everard fleet to carry the name, but her predecessors were built in less exotic climes. Built in Wuhan in China, at the Qingshan Shipyard, this ship is the first of a planned group of four sisterships, and will be followed by the **Seniority**, **Superiority** and the **Supremity**. A twin-engined double-hulled tanker with a deadweight tonnage of 4,426 tonnes, her cargo is carried in six coated cargo tanks, each of which is fitted with a deepwell pump for discharge purposes.     (M)

In an average year about 800 voyages will be conducted at the port by vessels in the 5,000-25,000 dwt range. These vessels, the small general purpose tankers, are to some extent the inheritors of the mantle of the famous wartime T2 tankers. At the port this sector is dominated by fleets from northern Europe, but there is an important British player in the form of the James Fisher Group of Barrow, and far from shrinking, they are growing especially since the merger with the Everard company to form James Fisher Everard. The **Clyde Fisher** (BHS, 8446gt/05) which appeared at the port in April 2005, is the second of two sisterships built at the Samho shipyard at Tongyoung in South Korea for the carriage of refined products. (M)

If the **Clyde Fisher** is at the start of her career at the port, the **Linnea** (NIS, 6972gt/80) has just come to the end of hers. Built as the **Hydro** at the Trosvik Verksted yard in Brevik, she was lengthened in 1984 at Tonsberg to bring her to the size shown here of 11,520 dwt. In 1988, she was sold by her owners, Norsk Hydro, to the Swedish company Vaderotank, under whose ownership she became the **Linnea**, though she retained her Norwegian registry. For almost 20 years she carried refined products from Milford Haven to the larger west coast and Irish ports such as Avonmouth, Dublin and Belfast. (M)

One of the major players in this sector is the Rigel company of Bremen with the distinctive "Stern" suffixes to the names and the six-pointed star on their funnels. The **Ledastern** (IOM, 6262gt/93), at 10,500 dwt is the "baby" of the fleet, and is one of a fairly large series of ships built for the company by the MTW yard at Wismar in Germany. The distinctive "Maerform" bow and the "triple foremast" arrangement make the class instantly recognisable. In 2005, at a service speed of about 12 knots, she moved about 80 cargoes from the port, mainly up the Irish Sea to Belfast.     (M)

In the 5,000 to 25,000 dwt product tanker sector, the Broström fleet, a Franco/Swedish venture as will be explained on page 13, is a major force and most days will see a ship of that fleet in the port. It is a rapidly expanding fleet and in early 2007 controlled about seventy ships. The **Bro Developer** (SWE, 11344gt/07), seen here in the process of berthing on to the Semlogistics Number 3 berth at Waterston, is the last in a series of four "D" class ships ordered and built at the Jinling Shipyard at Nanjing in China. From the coastal path above the terminal it is possible to get a grandstand view of such operations.     (E)

It is difficult to talk about the Swedish mercantile marine without making reference to the port of Donsö, on an island near the city of Gothenburg. This island appears to the outsider to be the port of registry of more than its fair share of Swedish-registered vessels. The **Prospero** (SWE, 11793gt/00) is one such ship. But that is not the only complicated matter for this ship, which was built at the Shanghai Edward Shipyard in 2000 for Partrederiet M/T Prospero. She is a diesel electric ship in which the normal method of propulsion - motor, shaft and propeller - is replaced by two azimuth electric drive units, power for which is provided by four 9-cylinder diesel generators providing power to a 6,900 hp electric motor.     (M)

The **Songa Maya** (MHL, 10948gt/88) was built for the Soviet merchant marine as the **Kapitan Rudnyev**. She was one of the 20 or more ships of the 17,500 dwt Josep Broz Tito class, all of which were constructed in Yugoslavian yards, and many of which were to become regular visitors to Milford Haven. Built at the Brodogradiliste Uljanik yard at Pula, she was powered by a Burmeister and Wain diesel engine built under licence at Pula. During the upheavals that occurred in the USSR in the 1990s, she was flagged out to Cyprus as the **Lake Maya**. In 2005 she was acquired by the Norwegian Blystad Group and renamed **Songa Maya**.     (A)

The "Bro" fleet, many of whose ships regularly use the waterway, was created by an amalgamation of the fleets of the Swedish Broström group and the French Soflumar Group. The **Bro Bara** (FRA, 17699gt/82) came from that latter fleet. She was built by the major Japanese shipbuilding company Ishikawajima Harima Heavy Industries at their Kure yard. Whilst in most outward aspects she was a perfectly routine vessel, in her cargo handling arrangements she was somewhat unusual in that she had only two cargo handling pumps. The photograph, showing the ship working cargo on the Chevron Number 2 berth, was taken from the decks of the **Isle of Inishmore** as she passed up the Haven on her way from Rosslare.    (N)

The tanker fleet operated by the Carl Büttner organisation of Bremen is a major force in European waters and their distinctive vessels, each named after a fish and with a painting of that fish on the front of the superstructure, are frequent visitors to the Haven. In recent years, the size of ship operated by them has increased so that the average Büttner ship is now about 30,000 dwt. Unlike many other European ship owners who have taken their business to the Far East, they still support their national shipbuilders. Büttner ships almost always come from the Lindenau yard at Kiel, and not surprisingly, as a result all look alike, good looking, workmanlike ships. The **Seadevil** (DEU, 21367gt/96) is no exception.    (E)

In 1976, the Kherson Shipyard in the Ukraine launched a 27,500 dwt product tanker for the Soviet merchant marine, the **Komandarm Fedko**. In so doing they created the first of what was to be a very long series of distinctive ships, many of which have visited the port over the years. Cargo cranes have replaced kingposts, the focsle has disappeared, and the internal structure has altered to accommodate the double hull requirement laws. But the basic look remains unchanged and as distinctive as ever. The **Wave A** (MLT, 21145gt/95), which was launched as **Capella** and one of the third generation ships of this series, was until recently operated by the Russian Prisco fleet of Nakhodka in the Russian Far East.    (A)

Some ship profiles leave doubt as to the ship's place of origin. Others shout it aloud. The profile of the **Lawrence H Gianella** (USA, 21471gt/86) shouts "US built". She was indeed built for the Wilmington Trust Company of Delaware, in two parts, the after section at Tampa in Florida, and the forward cargo section at Avondale in Louisiana. The funnel colours say that she is a Military Sealift Command ship, built for the carriage of fuel for the US forces. If emphasis of that fact is needed, it is provided by the sight of the port side replenishment at sea gantries. A 5-cylinder Sulzer engine built by the IHI works at Aioi in Japan provides the 11,200 hp necessary to drive this 32,970 dwt tanker at a service speed of 16 knots.    (A)

Whilst the Middle East may be the origin of much of the traded oil in the world today, at Milford Haven, cargoes with a Middle Eastern origin are relatively rare, and ships with a Middle Eastern ownership are even rarer. The **Dukhan** (QAT, 25408gt/03) is an exception to that rule, being owned by Q Ships, the Qatar Shipping Company, and is registered in Doha. A 37,200 dwt product tanker, she is one of three sisterships built for the company by the Shin A Shipbuilding Company of Tongyoung in South Korea, one of the lesser-known Korean yards. The picture, taken from the coastal path above the beach at Pwllcrochan, shows her loading cargo for New York at the Semlogistics Terminal.    (L)

A very distinctive ship in distinctive funnel colours. Very few shipyards build kingposts for the hose handling derricks with such heavy crosstrees. The Japanese yard Koyo Dockyard at Mihara was one such yard and they built and launched this 41,500 dwt product tanker as the **World Sea** for the Worldwide Shipping Group. As if to add to the individuality of the ship, instead of the routine two kingposts she carries just a single kingpost on her main deck. In 2004 she was named **Rangoon** (SGP, 25740gt/89) when she was acquired by the Singaporean company Tanker Pacific Management, in whose very distinctive gold band on blue funnel colours the ship is seen being swung onto the Semlogistics No 2 berth by the tugs **Millgarth** and **Svitzer Milford**.     (E)

Ships in the 30,000 to 50,000 dwt range, medium range tankers, constitute the major movers in the import and export of oil product cargoes, often over long distances, and particularly so in the export trade to the USA. The **Timashevsk** (LBR, 26218gt/96) is a typical ship in this latter trade. Built for the Novorossiysk Shipping Corporation, this 40,500 dwt tanker is a regular visitor to the port, loading refined products for the USA, making ten calls in 2005. The very distinctive trellis foremast is a clue that the ship might have been built in the Adriatic, as indeed she was, having been constructed at the "3 Maj" Brodogradiliste Yard in Rijeka.     (A)

The **Hellas Serenity** (GRC, 27645/99) was a pretty unremarkable medium range tanker, built at the Ulsan yard of Hyundai Heavy Industries. Built for Montagu Marine SA of Piraeus, she had a deadweight tonnage of 46,168 tonnes and a Hyundai built B&W diesel engine of 10,500 hp gave her a speed of about 14 knots. More interestingly, this photograph is almost certainly the last one taken of the ship under that name, because she is leaving the port to go to St Brides Bay where she underwent a name change. She had been sold to the Top Tanker Management Inc who renamed her **Soundless** and placed her under the flag of the Marshall Islands.     (A)

The *Cariad* (BRB, 28337gt/96) is a representative of another fleet commonly employed in the transatlantic trade in fuel to the USA. Built at the Sestao yard of the Astilleros Espanoles S.A., she has a deadweight of about 45,000 tonnes. A Manises-built 5-cylinder B&W diesel gives her a service speed of about 14 knots. She is owned by the Admanthos Shipping group of Stamford, Connecticut, started life as the *Libertad*, but was renamed *Cariad* in 2000. Ships in the Admanthos Group all bear names ending in "ad", though probably few of the crew know that their ship's name is Welsh for "*Sweetheart*". Maybe a good thing!     (M)

A/S Dampskibsselskabet Torm, or Torm Lines of Copenhagen, is another major Danish operator in the oil trades, with more than 30 tankers, all over 40,000 tonnes deadweight, listed under its name in 2007. It has also been around for a long time, having been established in 1899. The *Torm Mary* (DIS, 30058gt/02), here seen being swung onto the Semlogistics Number 2 berth after arriving from Rotterdam, was built by the STX Shipbuilding Company Ltd at Chinhae in South Korea, a yard that, though quite new, has made something of a name for itself in building these medium-sized product tankers.     (E)

The *Jill Jacob* (CYM, 40037gt/03), built at the Koje yard of Samsung Shipbuilding and Heavy Industries in South Korea, is a Far Eastern built example of a larger range product tanker. Built as their Yard Number 1422, this 72,999 dwt tanker was originally named *Four Clipper*. In 2004, she was acquired by Ernst Jacob GmbH & Co KG of Flensburg and renamed *Jill Jacob*. She joined a fleet of twelve other tankers in that organisation, all but one of which are large ships in the range of 60,000 to 160,0000 dwt. The photo shows her outbound with 65,000 tonnes of heavy fuel oil for New York.    (A)

With the growth of tanker shipping worldwide, and with it the rise of new shipping companies, it is inevitable that ships will arrive at the port owned by lines hitherto unseen. The *New Champion* (MHL, 41994gt/05) is one such ship. Owned by the CNC Shipping Corporation and managed by Expedo Ship Management (Canada) Ltd of Ontario, she was built by the New Century Shipbuilding Co Ltd of Jingjiang in China, a shipyard which has only been building ships since 2002, yet by 2006 had already thirty major vessels to its credit. The compact superstructure and the pole foremast produces a tanker profile generally associated with ships built at a number of Chinese yards.    (A)

The **Siboelf** (NIS, 41189gt/93), as an ore/bulk/oil carrier, is an example of a class of ships which found great favour in certain quarters in the 1980s and 1990s as a means of producing a very flexible bulk carrier capable of carrying both dry and liquid cargoes. Higher than expected maintenance costs would take some of the shine off the success of this innovative idea. This 74,868 dwt example of the type was built at the Copenhagen yard of Burmeister and Wain and was managed by Tschudi and Eitzen Ship Management (Singapore) Pte Ltd. Dry cargo is carried in nine oil tight holds of which the large hatches can be seen on the main deck.     (A)

Of the larger product tankers arriving in the port in 2005, the vast majority were built in European yards, particularly in Scandinavian yards. The **Loyalty** (PAN, 43363gt/85) was an example of the output of such yards. This rather unusual looking ship, with the heavy main deck strengthening and the cutaway quarterdeck was built as the **Toluma** by the Uddevalla yard in Sweden for K/S A/S Tabriz and managed by the famous Wilhelmsen company of Tonsberg in Norway. In 1993 she was acquired by the large Wallem organisation and now sails under the Panamanian flag. With cargo heating capacity and a cargo pump in each tank, she is a very flexible cargo carrying ship.     (M)

Loading at the Semlogistics Number 2 Terminal is the veteran large tanker **Kirsten** (NIS, 44322gt/88). The trellis type foremast again suggests an Adriatic origin, and so it is, for she was built, as **Georgia**, at the Brodogradiliste "3 Maj" Yard at Rijeka in Croatia. After a series of ownership and name changes, she is now managed by the Thome Ship Management Pte Ltd, a company of Norwegian origin, but with a major ship management operation in Singapore as well as in Scandinavia. Having arrived from Rotterdam in ballast, the ship is loading 58,000 tonnes of oil products for New York. Movements across the Atlantic to the East coast of the USA of clean product cargoes of this size are quite routine matters at the port.    (E)

With the growth of producer country refining capacity, long gone are the days when one could assume that any tanker over 70,000 dwt must be a crude oil carrier. Each year the port is visited by a number of large vessels in the 70,000 to 100,000 tonne range which import or export cargoes of refined products. The establishment of a storage terminal at the old Gulf refinery has increased the trade in products. The **Sara Viking** (NIS, 43398gt/90) is one of a series of 84,000 dwt tankers built in Copenhagen by Burmeister & Wain to meet the demand for large product carriers. Owned by Waterfront Shipping Co of Oslo, she is now managed by TESMA Denmark A/S, a ship management company with worldwide connections.    (M)

The bulk of crude oil arriving at the port, regardless of reports of declining supplies from that area, still arrives from the North Sea. Some of it is transhipped from ports on the east coast of the UK, the Tees being a major loading port. The **Forward Pioneer** (PAN, 58099gt/05) is one of the vessels associated with that trade. Built at the Mihara yard of the Koyo Dockyard Company, she is a typical product of that yard. A 107,081 dwt vessel, she is owned by the San Clemente Shipping Company of Panama, but two red bands on a white banded funnel indicate that, whatever her brass plate ownership, she is in fact part of the NYK organisation/Mitsubishi Group. (A)

Outwardly a very ordinary ship to be operating on the North Sea run, a standard 115,000 tonne tanker built by Daewoo Heavy Industries at Okpo in South Korea, the **Penelop** (BHS, 63448gt/06) is owned by a company coming from an area with a long and distinguished history of seafaring. Though registered in the Bahamas, the ship is owned by Lundqvist Rederierna AB, of Mariehamn on the Åland Islands, the Finnish islands located at the mouth of the Gulf of Bothnia in the Baltic. The Lundqvist company was established in 1927 and though it has been active in a number of trades, it presently confines its activities to the oil trades running a fleet of eight modern tankers, all of similar dimensions to that of the **Penelop**. (A)

The growth of North Sea oil fields brought with it the rise of the complex shuttle tanker capable of loading from terminals in deep water, often in very inhospitable conditions. This sector the Norwegian companies have made their own. The **Grena** (BHS, 81141gt/03) is an example of the latest technology in this area. Built at the Koje Island yard of Samsung Heavy Industries in Korea, this 148,553 dwt tanker is seen in the colours of the J Ludwig Mowinckel company of Bergen. She has bow thrusters, stern thrusters and a retractable azimuthing thruster to hold her on station whilst loading offshore. A B&W diesel of 23,000 hp produces a service speed of nearly 15 knots.    (M)

The Ugland organisation of Grimstad in Norway is another important operator in the shuttle tanker sector. The **Gerrita** (NIS, 60866gt/90), seen here discharging at the Number 6 berth at the Chevron Refinery, is an example of a Spanish-built shuttle tanker, having been built at the Sestao Yard of Astilleros Espanoles SA. With a deadweight of 112,000 tonnes, she is one of the smaller ships in this sector. A single 5-cylinder engine producing some 14,600 hp drives the ship along at a service speed of about 14 knots. Since the photo was taken the ship has been taken in hand for conversion to a Floating Offshore Production Unit which will in turn load cargoes into other shuttle tankers.    (N)

The Knutsen company of Haugesund in western Norway is one of the principal operators of shuttle tankers. Their red-hulled vessels with the distinctive black funnel with two red bands are to be seen at the port every week. The **Karen Knutsen** (IOM, 88109gt/99) is somewhat unusual in that she started life at the Ulsan yard of Hyundai Heavy Industries as a routine crude oil carrier, the **Knock Whillan**. However, she was then converted into a shuttle tanker at the same yard by the addition of the bow loading gear, which is obvious in the photograph, and by the addition of a number of thrusters deep below the waterline to enable the ship to hold station whilst loading at deepwater oil terminals in the often stormy North Sea.    (A)

Norwegian shipowners are amongst the most innovative in the world, and the **Odin** (NIS, 65878gt/01) typifies this spirit. This "back to front" tanker with the accommodation block in the bow, is probably one of very few tankers of this kind in the world. Built at the Puerto Real yard of the Spanish Izar Construcciones Navales SA as the **Navion Odin** for Rasmussen Maritime Services A/S, this multi-purpose shuttle tanker of 96,000 dwt visited the port only once. Whether the innovative design would stand the test of time we will never know, for she was acquired in 2006 to be converted at the Haugesund shipyard into a Floating Production and Storage Unit for the Norwegian sector Alvheim Field.    (A)

Whilst the North Sea provides the bulk of the port's imported crude oil, cargoes also arrive from more distant areas. The Chevron Group has important commercial connections in equatorial Africa and has adapted its Pembroke refinery to be able to use crude oil from Komo Kribi in Cameroon. Such cargoes will routinely arrive in very large tankers. The **SCF Khibiny** (LBR, 81985gt/02), a 159,196 dwt tanker, was built at the Ulsan yard of Hyundai Heavy Industries as their Yard Number 1335 for the Wilshire Corporation. This company is an owning vehicle for ships managed by the Russian SCF Group, Sovcomflot Akp of Moscow, a group which, after the economic chaos of the 1990s in Russia, is now beginning to invest heavily in new tonnage.     (A)

Long-haul crude brings with it the prospect of unusual vessels and unfamiliar owners. The **Voyager** (MHL, 79525gt/01), at 149,991 dwt, though not strictly a VLCC, is by any standards a very large ship. Built by the renowned Sasebo Heavy Industries in Japan, which was one of the great names in the heyday of Japanese shipbuilding, the **Voyager** was built for the Glyn Enterprises Company. A 6-cylinder B&W diesel producing 16,820 bhp gives a service speed of about 15 knots and the three cargo pumps can discharge the cargo at a rate of 10,500 tonnes per hour.     (D)

An integral part of oil refining is the use and production of liquefied petroleum gas (LPG), principally butane and propane. Butane is received in small parcels from UK and other European sources. Propane, butane and other gases are produced and shipped to markets in the UK, Eire, the Continent and North Africa. Almost all of the exported LPG is carried in small LPG carriers, some of them of less than 2,000 dwt. The **Gas Pioneer** (IOM, 1173gt/91) was a regular visitor in this trade and in 2005 moved more than sixty cargoes, mainly across the Irish Sea to Drogheda and Cork, but occasionally to Stornoway in the outer isles of Scotland, when the cargo might be of less than 500 tonnes.     (M)

It is almost impossible to talk about the small LPG ships using the waterway without making mention of the "Kosan" tankers. Kosangas of Denmark, owned by the Tholstrup family, pioneered the carriage of LPG in small ships and their small yellow gas tankers have been an integral part of the port's oil industry traffic since it first began in the 1960s. The **Tine Kosan** (DNK, 1395gt/68) was built for the company as **Tine Tholstrup** by Jos L Meyer, of Papenburg, a German shipbuilder which went on to establish a fine reputation as a builder of gas tankers and later of much larger cruise ships.     (K)

Butane arrives at the port in small parcels from ports on the east coast of the UK, from Norway and occasionally from Germany. One of the vessels participating in this trade in 2006 was the 6,175 deadweight tonne *Epsilongas* (ATG, 5278gt/00). One of the vessels of the Bremen-based Sloman fleet, her hull was built at the Santierul Naval yard at Constanta in Romania and was completed at the Mützelfeldtwerft shipyard in Cuxhaven on the River Elbe. She is shown wearing the funnel colours of the Unigas Consortium and departing via the Western Channel having delivered 5,200 tonnes of butane to the Chevron refinery from Grangemouth in Scotland.    (A)

The shipping world is one of constant change. Fleets come and go, grow and shrink. In the LPG world, 2005 witnessed the emergence of a new fleet in the trade when the Greek company Stealthgas Inc arrived on the scene, and by 2006 was announcing its expansion to a fleet of 24 vessels. The *Gas Legacy* (CYP, 3392gt/98) was the first ship of that fleet to visit the port. She started life as the *Regulus Gas*, having been built at Usuki by Shitanoe Zosen KK as their Yard Number 1202 for Viking Carriers of Panama. In 2002 she became *Arago* owned by the Swan Shipping Corp of Tonga, and in 2006 the 3,318 dwt tanker was acquired by Stealthgas.    (M)

Until recently, the shipyards of the south eastern European countries primarily built relatively unsophisticated dry cargo ships or ships' hulls, which were then sent for completion in the yards of western Europe. Such a state of affairs no longer holds true as the photo shows. The **Saargas** (LBR, 3932gt/01), a twin-tank pressurised LPG carrier and a quite sophisticated ship by any measure, was built at the Societatea Comerciala Severnav SA at Drobeta-Turnu Severin on the River Danube in Romania. She is owned by the Avelina Shipping Co of Liberia and managed by Donnelly Tanker Management Ltd, an important player in the world of ship management.    (M)

Though there may be little room for sentiment in business, the demise of the "Kosan" name was a milestone in the history of lpg shipping. In 1989, Kosan tankers was taken over by another Danish shipping company, the long-established J Lauritzen Group though the Kosan name was retained for the gas tanker fleet. The **Linda Kosan**, was built for this Group at the Hermann Sürken shipyard in Papenburg. In 2006 the ship was sold, along with eight other small gas tankers, to another long-established shipping company, the Eitzen Group, and her name was changed to **Sigas Linda** (SGP, 2224gt/92). The long history of the small yellow gas tankers at the port will end when her hull colour is changed to the bright red of the Eitzen fleet.    (A)

Whilst small parcels of LPG are both imported and exported by the port's refineries, the trade in LPG in parcels of in excess of 10,000 tonnes is exclusively an import trade. The principal sources of such cargoes are Braefoot Bay in Scotland, and the Norwegian mainland terminals such as Mongstad and Karsto. For many years the LPG import trade has been dominated by the immaculate green-hulled ships of the Bergesen fleet from Oslo. Of the 36 large butane cargoes received by the port in 2005, 15 were carried by the Bergesen sisterships **Helga** and **Hedda**. The **Helga** (NIS, 22521gt/94), built at the Kobe yard of Kawasaki Heavy Industries, carries her parcels of about 20,000 tonnes of butane in three independent tanks.     (A)

The huge Danish AP Møller shipping organisation is active in the world of LPG shipping and their gas carriers are regular visitors. **Jakob Mærsk** (DIS, 23878gt/91) was built at the Ulsan yard of Hyundai Heavy Industries as their Yard Number 670, one of four "J" class gas tankers built for the A/S D/S Svendborg & D/S of 1912 A/S. Her four cargo tanks, with a capacity of about 35,000 cubic metres, are capable of carrying a range of liquefied gases in a refrigerated state. Since this picture was taken, all four ships have been sold and **Jakob Mærsk** now sails under the name of **Maharshi Bhavatreya** for VSC International Pte Ltd of Singapore, part of the Varun Shipping Co Ltd, of Mumbai in India.     (A)

In 2005, the large parcel LPG trade, which had been the preserve of Scandinavian shipping fleets, saw the arrival of a new operator, Navigator Gas Transport, whose ships were on long-term time charter to the Italian company Montenari. The *Navigator Neptune* (LBR, 17840gt/00), built at the Jiangnan shipyard in Shanghai, also introduced Chinese-built LPG ships to the port. A Sulzer diesel engine of 13,050 hp gives a service speed of 16.5 knots for this 23,495 dwt LPG carrier. Her cargo is carried in four independent horizontal tanks with a capacity of about 22,000 cubic metres. Whilst the ship was novel, the cargo, from Norway, was completely routine.    (A)

The *Berge Flanders* (BHS, 42286gt/91) visited the port only once in 2005, but the ship and source of her cargo justify her inclusion. At 49,345 tonnes deadweight, she is much larger than the routine LPG carriers visiting the port. She started life as the *Tsugaru Gloria*, built at the Sakaide Yard of Kawasaki Heavy Industries. In 1996, she became the *Gloria*, in 1997 the *Flanders Gloria*, and in 2003, the *Berge Flanders*. She has four cargo tanks with a capacity of 75,353 cubic metres. Her cargo reputedly came from Bahia Blanca in Argentina, over 6,000 miles from the Haven.    (A)

Geography and history have ensured that there would be an Irish connection at the waterway. In centuries past, the Haven was used as a staging post for the movement of people, goods, and armies to and from Ireland. In the 19th century, there were attempts to create ferry services from Neyland by persons as illustrious as Isambard Kingdom Brunel, but to no avail. In 1978, however, the "Irish Ferry" returned to the Haven when British and Irish Ferries began operating from a newly-constructed terminal at Pembroke Dock. The vessel presently dedicated to the route is the *Isle of Inishmore* (CYP, 34031gt/97). Built at Krimpen a/d IJssel by Van der Giessen and with a capacity of 800 cars, 122 lorries and 1,992 passengers, she maintains a twice-daily service to Rosslare at a service speed of about 21 knots.      (E)

The *Isle of Inishmore* has proven to be a remarkably reliable ship and, inclement weather and errant passengers notwithstanding, she maintains a regular service from Pembroke Dock. However, surveys and refits require that she spends time in dry dock, or time at Holyhead deputising for other vessels in the fleet. On such occasions, replacement craft are chartered in to maintain the service. So, every January or February, a replacement ferry will appear. The *Leili* (CYP, 7606gt/99) was one such vessel. A "freight-only" ferry, she was built at Huelva in Spain and is owned by the Estonian Shipping Company. Twin Wärtsilä diesels give her a service speed of 17 knots.     (A)

To the south of the waterway is the British army's Armoured Vehicle Training Range at Castlemartin, an area used not only by British troops but by our Nato allies. The ferry port at Pembroke Dock becomes their port of entry, and, as a result will play host to some exotic ships and cargoes. The **Boa Vista** (PAN, 8104gt/73), built at Capelle a/d IJssel in The Netherlands and seen here approaching the ferry terminal, has had an "interesting" career, at least ten previous names, several conversions, a lengthening, and service on both sides of the Atlantic. She was chartered to move vehicles of the Belgian army, the personnel arriving by road. Not serving any specific routes, she continues to serve as a general purpose ferry .    (K)

Given the fact that the Castlemartin range is the British army's principal live firing tank range, it is hardly surprising that vessels will appear in the waterway from the Strategic Sealift Service. The **Hurst Point** (GBR, 23235gt/02), seen here leaving the Irish ferry terminal, is one of a class of six vessels built for this service. She was built, along with three others, at the Flensburg shipyard in Germany. Unlike most support vessels, the class is operated outside the RFA service under a Private Funding Initiative (PFI) contract with AWSR Shipping Ltd, probably better known as Andrew Weir & Co. She is capable of carrying 25 main battle tanks, 25 personnel carriers, plus artillery and trucks, at a service speed of about 17 knots.    (G)

In what was once the largest ship-owning country in the world, today 44 tonne juggernauts have fan clubs and the number of ship owning companies dwindles yearly. Yet, properly managed, water transport is still the most cost-efficient way of moving goods. And so the port continues to receive a small number of dry cargo ships each year. As befits an area where there is a vast acreage of metal to be painted and maintained, cargoes of blasting grit will be imported from Dordrecht in parcels of about 1,000 tonnes. For cargoes of this size, the **Borelly** (GBR, 571gt/71) fits the bill exactly. Built at Wartena in Holland as the **Jana Weston**, she was renamed in 1984. Unlike some ageing UK dry cargo coasters, she remained in British ownership and under the British flag until sold in late 2007.    (K)

In the 1970s and 1980s, the Soviet merchant marine built huge classes of small coasters, many of which can still be seen actively trading. **Vasiliy Shukshin** (RUS, 2264gt/95) is one of the successors to this huge fleet. Built at Volgograd by the Volgogradskiy Sudostroitelnyy Zavod yard, she is one of many vessels managed by the North Western Shipping Joint Stock Company of St Petersburg. A 2,366 hp Wärtsilä engine produces a service speed of about 12 knots. Her cargo here is of Baltic timber, which, because of its relatively low density, will require a significant element to be carried as deck cargo to bring the ship down to her loading marks.    (M)

In days when British ship owning companies are fast disappearing, the **Silver River** was a welcome kick against the trend. The owning company, Mezeron, is based in the Isle of Man and in 2006 operated two dry cargo ships. The **Silver River** (IOM, 277gt/68) was built at Oldersum in Germany and with a gross tonnage of 277 tonnes and a deadweight of only 373 tonnes, she was probably the smallest cargo vessel to use the waterway in 2005. Trading normally in the Irish Sea, she appeared at the Port of Pembroke to load a prefabricated superstructure for a vessel being converted in a Ramsey shipyard.    (M)

The most easterly commercial berth in the waterway is the Waterloo Quay berth where ships load large pieces of equipment, often for oil-related industries, constructed by engineering firms based principally in the town of Pembroke Dock. The photo shows the **Aqua Star** (ATG, 1507gt/79) arriving to berth on the high tide. She is assisted by the small tugs **Lilah** at her bow, and **Seamaid** at her stern. Built at the Wewelsfleth yard of Hugo Peters, she was owned by Aqua Blue Bereederung GmbH of Hamburg. She will take the ground as the tide falls, and later, when the tide rises, she will load a heat exchanger for a Norwegian oil refinery.    (J)

To reach Waterloo Quay, ships must pass under the Cleddau Bridge. Very occasionally all the pieces fall into place - ship, light, time - and the result is a picture for the record book. The small coaster *Embla* (DIS, 699gt/68), seen here in the June sunshine, is arriving in ballast to load a hot oil furnace built at the Ledwood Engineering works for an oil refinery in Norway. She was built at Mandal in Norway and well built too, for when this photograph was taken in 1995, she was already almost 30 years old. She was still trading in 2002, when she retired to the sun and was sold to owners in Madagascar. (H)

2005 brought confirmation that the port would be developed to accept the import of Liquefied Natural Gas (LNG) and construction work began on two sites, one at South Hook, one at Waterston, to the east and west of the town of Milford Haven. With the construction vessels that began to congregate, there came a number of imported cargoes of materials. The *Aura* (ATG 2416gt/92) brought a cargo of steel piles to the South Hook site and, when part discharged, the weather broke. The photo shows her running for sea room to ride out the storm. A coaster with a difference, she was built as the *Jens* at Budapest in the Ganz Danubus Shipyard and Crane Factory, and is now owned by Berend Meyering Schiffahrts KG of Haren on the Ems River in Germany. (A)

Whilst Waterloo Quay is the uppermost berth on the Milford waterway, such a location can be no strange thing to the **Denika** (ATG, 1495gt/78). Built as the **Merlan**, this ship started life in one of the lesser known German shipyards, at the Bayerische Schiffbau yard, at Erlenbach, a town on the River Main in central Germany, and many miles from the sea. When photographed in 1998, she was owned by Reederei Frank Dahl of Stade on the River Elbe, and is seen in the process of loading a large unit for shipment to the Netherlands. The growth of engineering companies in the latter part of the 20th century close to this inlet led to the construction of this berth to accommodate their transport needs.     (J)

Seen here unloading a cargo of steel plate from Oslo at the Port of Pembroke Number 1 Quay, the coaster **Inkeri** (NLD, 2787gt/73) was built by one of the most productive and famous dry cargo shipbuilders in western Europe, J J Sietas of Hamburg. The distinctive "chunky" superstructure is a typical characteristic of a Sietas ship. Built as the **Sagitta**, the ship has been through a procession of names and owners, though is now owned by Helen Laiva BV and registered in Rotterdam. She is powered by a German MaK engine, an engine that appears to find particular favour with the Sietas company.     (K)

In the first half of the 20th century, Milford Haven was one of the UK's leading fishing ports. Over-fishing, rising costs, and the EU have put an end to much of this nationwide. With it went much of the UK's fishing vessel building industry. Today the sight of a British-built fishing boat of any size in Milford Haven is a rare thing indeed. *Mercurius* (GBR, 86gt/63) represents one of the few remaining locally-owned fishing vessels, though she was built in Belgium as *Sandra*. She is a small beam trawler operating on the near water fishing grounds, landing her catch at the port for sale through the local fish merchanting organisations.     (C)

The south-west of England still possesses a fishing industry, albeit reduced, and vessels from that area are not only quite frequent visitors to the port, but also avail themselves of the port's dry docking facilities. The *Cheryl of Ladram* (GBR, 232gt/80) started life as the *Grietje*, built at Foxhol in the Netherlands by Scheepswerf Bodewes Gruno BV, a yard much more famous for its dry cargo ships. A beam trawler, she has had a number of owners, adopting her present name in 2006 whilst under refit with the Milford Haven Ship Repairers.     (B)

Like most UK ports, the waterway is home to an active shell fishing industry, carried out almost entirely by small inshore craft and principally catching crustaceans. However, other sections of the shell fish industry occasionally bring to the port vessels which are as distinctive as they are unusual. The **Schillhorn** (DEU, 156gt/81), here seen discharging a cargo of cockles in Milford Docks, in real life is a shell fish dredger. Built by Schiffswerft Gebr Schlömer at Oldersum in Germany and owned by the Gerjets Muschelzucht und Fischereigesellschaft of Hooksiel, she is seen here acting as a simple cargo carrier. The rules under which the cockle beds in Carmarthen Bay are harvested do not allow the use of mechanised fishing. So she has been relegated to use as a floating collection service.     (B)

Another shell fishery of note on the west coast of the UK is the scallop fishery of the northern Irish Sea. The **Albion** (GBR, 375gt/85), here seen entering Milford Docks to land her catch on 19 October 2006, is from that area, being owned by A J Scott of Dumfries. Like many UK fishing vessels built in the latter years of the 20th century, she was built overseas, and, in the case of the **Albion**, she was built as **De Kaper** at the Zeebrugge yard of NV Scheepswerven L de Graeve, a yard which has built many of the Belgian beam trawlers which visit the port. The individual dredges which make up the catching gear can be seen draped over the gunwhales.     (C)

In the latter years of the 20th century, a major part of the English and Welsh fishing industry passed into Spanish ownership. Whatever the rights and wrongs, the result was the movement of many elderly UK fishing vessels into Spanish ownership, often without change of name. The **Suffolk Endeavour** (GBR, 341gt/68), one such vessel, was built at Appledore for the famous East Anglian fishing company Small & Co. When EU fishing quotas began to bite, she was converted for use as a safety vessel in the North Sea oil industry. On acquisition by Spanish interests, she was converted back to a side trawler and as such she became a regular visitor to the port.     (C)

The arrival of Spanish-owned companies in British fishing ports also introduced to Britain vessels with "more exotic" backgrounds such as the **Bergur** (GBR, 250gt/65). Built at VEB Elbewerft at Boizenburg, which in 1965, was in East Germany, she has been through a succession of owners, names and fishing registers. Built for Icelandic owners, she joined the Fleetwood fish producers organisation and was registered at Fleetwood as the **Bergur Vigeus** in 2002. She is technically known as a liner and has been fishing principally for sharks. Interestingly, though built at the height of the Cold War, she appears to have been built with a British Lister Blackstone engine.     (C)

One of the newest vessels of the "Anglo Spanish" fishing fleet is the **Gonpez I** (GBR, 271gt/03), owned by Pesquera Gonzamar SL, a Spanish company, though she is registered at Falmouth, as the fishing number painted on her hull shows. Built at Marin, north of Vigo in Galicia by the Factoria Naval de Marin, one of the more important fishing vessel builders in Spain, she is a stern trawler, handling her fishing gear with the gantry at the stern of the vessel. Such an arrangement makes life considerably safer for the men on deck than the traditional side fishing method. The catch will be offloaded in the fish dock and taken by lorry back to the Spanish markets.    (C)

Occasionally the port plays host to a Spanish fishing vessel which belongs to what one might term the real Spanish fishing fleet, a vessel registered in Spain and carrying Spanish fishing register numbers. The **Nuevo Nemesia** (ESP, 393gt/00) was built at Burela by Astilleros Armon Burela SA, a yard which those who follow fishing matters would recognise as a leading Spanish fishing vessel builder. A stern trawler built for owners in Vigo, as the fishing numbers under the anchor show, she is powered by a Belgian built ABC diesel of 586 hp.    (C)

Whilst the UK and Anglo Spanish fleets may attract most attention, the Belgian fleet, principally from the port of Zeebrugge, is the largest and most active fleet using the port. In 2005, 54 vessels made about 240 calls at the port, March and April being the busiest months. The vessels range from very new large beam trawlers to quite diminutive vessels. *Zuiderzee* (BEL, 251gt/82) is one of the oldest, though most active Belgian beam trawlers, making 15 calls at the port in 2005. Built at Oostkamp, inland from Bruges, by Scheepswerven West Vlaamse, she is powered by a 1,050 hp Bolnes diesel engine.    (C)

Fishing vessel builders in northern Europe suffer the same pressures as the merchant shipbuilders and adopt the same responses, subcontracting out the hull building to lower cost areas and concentrating on the higher value fitting out work. The hull for the *Vaya Con Dios* (BEL, 351gt/99) was built in Gdansk in Poland and the ship completed at the Irnsum yard in Friesland in the north of The Netherlands for BVBA de Flamingo of Zeebrugge. As such she is one of the newer Belgian vessels to use the port. A 9-cylinder MaK engine producing 1,160 hp in a vessel of only 351 gt demonstrates the large motive power required by the beam trawl method of fishing.    (C)

Whilst the beam trawl method predominates in the visiting Belgian fishing fleet, vessels using other methods do call. The **Aegir** (BEL, 336gt/87) is one of those exceptions. A stern trawler, her profile contrasts markedly with that of her Belgian compatriots. She is also one of the more frequent visitors, making 16 calls in 2005. She was built in Ostend by Industrielle des Pecheries SV for NV Rederij Pieters, also of Ostend, where she is registered. She is powered by a Deutz engine of some 800 hp, which is markedly less powerful than the engines installed in beam trawlers of comparable size.     (C)

Each year, with the routine fishing fleet visitors to the Western Approaches, comes a contingent of small Belgian fishing vessels, often with gross tonnages of less than 100 gt, and overall lengths of less than 25 metres. One wonders what crazy system puts such small vessels in such big waters. The **Venus** (BEL, 98gt/88), owned by BVBA Rederij Vertrouwen of Zeebrugge is one such vessel. Built by the West Vlaamse Scheepswerven yard at Oostkamp near Bruges, she is fitted out as a beam trawler, though increasingly other small vessels are using the twin otter trawls to reduce power needs and fuel costs.     (C)

The worldwide cruise ship industry has grown rapidly in recent years and cruising in temperate waters has been one of the growth sectors. The Port Authority, mindful of the waterway's dependence on the oil industry, has consciously attempted, with a degree of success, to attract cruise ships to the port. The **Sea Cloud II** (MLT, 3849gt/00) was one of the more unusual of such vessels to arrive, and is from what one might term the "high value" end of the market. Built by Astilleros Gondan SA at Castropol in Spain for the German owners Schiffahrtsges "Hansa Columbus" GmbH, she is a powered sailing vessel, technically a barque, with berths for 96 passengers.    (F)

The **Black Prince** (BHS, 11209gt/66) is one of the much-loved veterans of the cruise ship industry, having been built as a combined ferry/cruise ship which adopted a cruising profile in the winter "off season" when ferry demand traditionally fell away. As a cruise ship she was called **Black Prince**; in the ferry mode she was **Venus** operating on the Newcastle to Bergen run. She was built by Lübecker Flender-Werke AG for Fred Olsen Lines of Oslo. In 1987 she was converted to a full cruise ship and now has 241 cabins with 451 berths. Twin Pielstick diesel engines give her a service speed of about 18.5 knots.    (F)

The **Saga Rose** (BHS, 24528gt/65), here seen at anchor on the Milford Shelf while her passengers explore the County, is yet another example of a niche market cruise ship, catering for a more elderly clientele. She was built to very high standards as the **Sagafjord** for the Norwegian America Line at the La Seyne yard of Forges et Chantiers de la Mediterranée. The exercise bankrupted the yard. Acquired by the Saga Shipping Company in 1997, she has become something of an institution in the cruise ship industry. With 325 cabins and 587 berths, she would be considered to be a small cruise ship by today's standards.    (D)

Hull and engines German-built, German-flagged, German-owned. Who says high-cost west Europeans cannot compete? The **Deutschland** (DEU, 22496gt/98), a medium-sized cruise ship with 600 berths, was built at the Howaldtswerke Deutsche Werft AG yard at Kiel for Peter Dielmann Rederei of Neustadt in Germany. Seen here anchored on the Milford Shelf, she was one of the cruise ships attracted to the waterway in 2006. With 600 passengers who could be comfortably accommodated by the facilities that the small towns of the hinterland have to provide, she fits neatly into the "upmarket profile" the Port Authority is seeking to promote.    (C)

Partly because of its sheltered anchorage on a rather inhospitable west coast, and maybe because the Port Authority looks kindly on such vessels, Milford Haven is a popular port of call for sailing craft, a number of which operate under the British flag as training vessels providing adventure, experience and character-building opportunities for able-bodied and disabled persons. The **Stavros S Niarchos** (GBR, 493gt/00), is one of the newer vessels operating in this sector. Operated by the Tall Ship Youth Trust, the twin-masted, square-rigged arrangement of sails means that she is classed as a brigantine, though hidden below for the days when the wind does not help, there are two modest diesel engines to provide auxiliary power.     (C)

In these days of utilitarian, and sometimes frankly rather ugly ships, the **Sedov** (RUS, 3432 gt/21) is one of those "takes your breath away" ships. A four-masted barque, square-rigged on the fore, main and mizzen masts, and fore and aft rigged on the after mizzen mast, she was built at Kiel by the Friedrich Krupp Germaniawerft as the **Magdalene Vinnen**. She is now owned by the Murmansk State Technical University in Russia and used as a training vessel for those seeking to enter the Russian Merchant Marine service. The photograph shows her being berthed in Milford Docks on a stopover visit which was to prove a major crowd puller.     (B)

Any major port in the UK will have a sand and aggregate terminal and Milford Haven plays host to such a unit at the Port of Pembroke, where approximately 30 to 35 cargoes of sand are received each year. The usual caller is the *City of Cardiff* (GBR, 2074gt/97), built by Appledore Shipbuilders for United Marine Dredging Ltd, and seen approaching No. 1 Quay in the Port of Pembroke. In tonnage terms, she is a small vessel of only 2,730 dwt, but in mechanical terms a complex vessel with suction loading and boom discharge unloading systems. Power for this twin-screw vessel is provided by a pair of 8-cylinder Wärtsilä diesels producing 3,700 hp.     (K)

Whilst the principal supplier of dredged sand at the port is the *City of Cardiff*, occasional visits are made by other sand vessels. Built in Sliedrecht by IHC Holland NV, probably the world's leading builder of such vessels, the *Arco Dart* (GBR, 1309 gt/90), shown in the photo in Milford Docks, is owned by Hanson Aggregates Marine Ltd, and one of the smaller vessels in that fleet. The self discharging system enables the full load to be discharged in less than six hours, making possible a turn around on a single tide at tidally-restricted ports and wharves but this is not necessary at the Port of Pembroke.     (B)

The port has had military and naval connections since English kings first appreciated the Haven's strategic importance on the route to Ireland. In the 19th century, Pembroke Dock was the site of an important naval dockyard. In the conflicts of the 20th century, it became a convoy assembly port. The naval base at Pembroke Dock is now limited to the storage of buoys and anchors. Not surprisingly, the principal naval vessels now to be seen in the port are the mooring and salvage vessels of the RMAS. The **Salmoor** (GBR, 2200displ/85) is one of a class of three mooring vessels built at the Aberdeen shipyard of Hall, Russell. Photographed outbound in the Haven's Western Channel, she is powered by a pair of 8-cylinder Ruston engines.　　(A)

With the closure of the naval tank farm and the removal of the historic **Warrior**, used as an oil hulk, to Hartlepool for restoration and permanent display in Portsmouth, Pembroke Dock ceased to be a naval bunkering port. The visit by the RFA tanker **Black Rover** (GBR, 7503gt/74) is thus an unusual event. Built as one of a class of five replenishment tankers, she has proved to be a remarkably versatile craft, even though the initial introduction of the class was marred by the installation of unproven engines. The ship is capable of carrying a range of cargoes and ship replenishment at sea. Small wonder that at 32 years old she is still scheduled to work for another four years.　　(G)

As befits a fishing port, the most common naval visitors are ships carrying the blue and yellow pennant of the Fishery Protection Squadron, often with a suitably chastened offending vessel following in the wake. In today's reduced Royal Navy, the task is carried out principally by the three River class ships which were built by the Vosper Thornycroft Group at Southampton, and are leased to the Navy under a PFI contract for use in the Squadron. **HMS Tyne** (GBR, 1700displ/02) was the first of the class to be delivered. Good looking ships, they have proved to be very efficient.     (F)

Ships attract sentiment unlike most industrial artefacts. None more so in the Principality of Wales than the **Sir Galahad** (GBR, 8900gt/87). This Landing Ship from the Royal Fleet Auxiliary was built at the Swan Hunter shipyard on the River Tyne to replace a vessel of the same name lost in the Falklands conflict whilst ferrying the Welsh Guards to Bluff Cove. The RNLI lifeboat built as an RFA memorial to that loss was allocated to the Tenby station and named **Sir Galahad**. Consequently, there is a very strong bond created between ship, RNLI and county of Pembrokeshire. The picture shows her arriving at Pembroke Dock naval base on a courtesy visit in June 2006.     (G)

The port occasionally receives calls from front line naval vessels and **HMS Montrose** (GBR, 3500displ/93), seen here running up the river towards the naval base at the Carr Jetty, is one such example. A Type 23 frigate, she is one of a class of 16 such vessels in the Royal Navy, in what is the biggest class of ships in the Navy since the building of the very successful Leander class of the 1960s. A combined diesel electric and gas turbine propulsion package provides the ability to produce both a high speed passage capacity and a slow speed, low noise submarine hunting ability. Harpoon and Seawolf missiles, torpedoes, and a 114 mm gun provide a powerful fighting capacity.    (F)

Naval Officers have to learn their trade somewhere and **HMS Express** (GBR, 43displ/88), one of the Archer Class training craft is where part of this, particularly the navigational skill, is achieved. The fourteen ships of this class are attached to the Royal Navy's University Unit, each one of the craft being dedicated to a University. The red dragon on the superstructure indicates that **Express** is the University of Wales's craft. Built in the 1980s, this one by the famous warship builder Vosper Thornycroft, these vessels have a permanent crew of five, but have accommodation sufficient for them to carry up to twelve trainees.    (C)

With the decision in 2005 to approve the construction of two LNG import terminals, one at South Hook for Esso/Mobil/Qatargas, the second at Waterston for British Gas/Petronas, to the west and east respectively of the town of Milford Haven, the nature of shipping movements on the waterway underwent a fundamental change. A whole host of workboats, tugs and construction craft descended upon the port and cargoes hitherto undreamed of began to move. One of the early arrivals was the workboat *Milo* (VCT, 160gt/89). Built as the **Knightbuster**, this 21-metre workboat is a product of the Damen company of Gorinchem. She would become the workhorse for the South Hook project.      (C)

Given the fact that the port construction and towage industries are much more developed on the Continent, and the main marine contractors for each LNG project came from that area, it was hardly surprising to find that many of the vessels, the construction barges and their attendant tugs also came from that part of the world, particularly the Low Countries. The tug *Indus* (NLD, 108gt/64) typified those vessels. Built by Wilton Fijenoord at Schiedam as the **Drydock I**, she became the **Smit Azie** in 1980. In 1990 she then became the *Indus* when she was acquired by Bouwman Marine of Zierikzee. In spite of her 33 years and no doubt much hard work, she remains in immaculate condition.      (C)

To move the enormous weights for the rebuilding of a pre-existing jetty at South Hook, the very large crane barge **Rambiz** (BEL, 6846gt/95) was employed. The vessel came into being as the result of the fusion in 1995 of two existing heavy lift pontoons, the **Ram** and the **Bison**, and hence the name. The pontoons were joined together by the Scheepswerf v/h P&A Ruijtenberg BV at Raamsdonksveer. The resulting creation has a lifting capacity of 2,750 tonnes. She is operated by Scaldis Salvage & Marine Contractors NV, a Belgian company with a worldwide reputation in this field.     (G)

The demolition of part of the old South Hook jetty generated large volumes of broken concrete and reinforcing steel which was processed on site in a storage barge called **Boa Barge 10**. To remove the product of this operation, a number of dry cargo coasters were chartered and the crushed concrete was sent to ports in the south-east of England. The **Helse** (ATG, 1582gt/92) was one such vessel. Completed at Büsum in Germany, she is owned by the energetic German coaster company Erwin Strahlmann of Hamburg, as part of a fleet which in 2006 numbered about 50 vessels.     (M)

Linking the import terminal with the UK gas mains network required the construction of a high pressure pipeline in excess of 100 miles long. The pipes to construct this line were brought by four ships, all sisterships, of the Volga Don Shipping Joint Stock Company of Taganrog in Russia. All four ships were built to a design by the Cassens shipyard at Emden in Germany. The **Voronezh** (RUS, 3796gt/96) was built entirely at that yard. The sisterships, **Aksay**, **Don** and **Temernik**, were built in part or in total at the Don Cassens Shipyard Ltd at Aksay in Russia, evidence of the movement of shipbuilding away from high cost yards in north-west Europe to cheaper ones in eastern Europe.     (F)

Given the volume and nature of construction work going on in the port in recent years, it is almost inevitable that we would see the **Mersey Mammoth** (GBR, 1793gt/86) in 2006. Built at Deest, upriver from Rotterdam, by the specialists in harbour plant construction, Scheepswerf Ravestein, this huge self-propelled floating crane, is owned by the Mersey Docks and Harbour Company of Liverpool. Though not the most sea-kindly of craft, her classification society arrangements allow her to undertake voyages around the UK in suitable weather conditions. In the photograph she is seen lifting sections of the discharge arm gantries, which she has carried down from the Port of Pembroke, into place on the newly-constructed Dragon LNG terminal.     (E)

2005 and 2006 saw the arrival of a whole host of specialised pieces of floating equipment for the LNG construction projects. Many came under their own power or by tow. But some pieces came from such distances that the only practical way for them to be moved was by specialist ships. The jack-up rig **Pauline** arrived from Equatorial Guinea in Africa on the load deck of the **Transshelf** (ANT, 26547gt/87), a semi-submersible ship built at the Wärtsilä Marine Industries yard at Turku in Finland. Loads are positioned by the simple expedient of sinking the ship under the intended cargo by taking in water ballast and then pumping out that ballast when the load has been floated into its correct position. Unloading is done by reversing the exercise.    (A)

Much of the assembled plant for the LNG projects was standard port construction equipment, although rarely, if ever, seen in the Haven. The **Shuttle 4** (VCT) and her three sisterships did not fit into that category. To cast the receiving terminal jetties at the South Hook project, large volumes of liquid concrete had to be moved to the site. This was achieved by using **Shuttle 4** and her sisters, specially designed self-propelled ready mixed concrete carriers, which would load large volumes of liquid concrete from a fleet of road vehicles which would arrive at Milford Docks pier head. Twin propulsion packages gave them the much-needed manoeuvring power.    (C)

There has been low level interest in exploration for oil and gas in the Celtic Sea for many years. In the Irish sector off Kinsale, Marathon Oil has successfully developed an offshore gas field. Continued interest in exploration and the proximity of the Kinsale Field means that the port plays host to a range of vessels working in this sector. The **Kommandor Jack** (BHS, 1318gt/61) a research and submersibles mother ship, started life as a stern trawler named **Vikingbank**, and anyone keen on fishing vessels could perhaps recognise her lines as a product of the famous AG Weser yard of Bremerhaven where she was built. She was converted to her present role in 1976.    (F)

Partly built in Poland and completed by Ulsteinverft AS, one of the world's leading builders of offshore supply ships at their yard in Norway, the **Olympic Pegasus** (NOR, 4477gt/02) is owned by Olympic Shipping AS of Fosnavåg, one of the younger companies in another sector which Norway has made its own. An anchor handling tug and supply ship, she is powered by four Wärtsilä diesels providing an incredible 23,492 hp. This gives a service speed of 17 knots and a bollard pull of 284 tonnes, more than the combined pulling power of the port's three tugs put together. For manoeuvring, she has four thrusters, two forward and two aft.    (F)

Built by Ørskov Christensens Staalskibsværft AS at Frederikshavn in Denmark for Farstad Shipping AS of Ålesund in Norway, the *Far Saltire* (IOM, 2642gt/02) is one of over seventy vessels in this very important offshore supply ship fleet. She demonstrates how large and powerful such vessels have become in recent years. Powered by four Normo diesels which produce 16,230 hp, she has a service speed of 16 knots and a bollard pull of 170 tonnes. In the supply ship mode she can carry a deck cargo of almost 1,000 tonnes.    (F)

Not all offshore vessels seen at the port are involved in oil and gas work. The *Prince Madog* (GBR, 390gt/01) represents those vessels which are involved in oceanographic research. The small North Wales port of Beaumaris has had a long connection with the oceanographic school of the University of Bangor and this is the latest vessel in that connection. Completed at the Den Helder yard of Scheepswerf Visser on a hull built in Romania, the vessel is actually owned by VT Ocean Sciences, a subsidiary of the Vosper Thornycroft group and is managed by VT Marine Services (Beaumaris) Ltd. In today's shipping world, nothing would appear to be simple!    (C)

The green and white cutters of the Milford Haven Port Authority are constantly visible on the waterway, moving pilots to ships and patrolling the waters. Larger than most UK pilot vessels because of the need to be able to handle the winds and waves of the Atlantic coast, the latest additions to the fleet were built locally at the Mustang Marine boatyard in Pembroke Dock. The **Robert Hastie**, the prototype fast cutter, was built in 2000 and is powered by twin MTU diesels producing some 1,600 hp. This large power pack provides speed of 20 knots when needed. The power and hull form enables the cutters to work in swell heights of up to five metres, conditions many other UK ports are normally spared.     (C)

The Port Authority operates a policy of tug escorts throughout the length of the Haven waterway for certain vessels, and to such duties, as well as the routine of berthing and unberthing ships, the tug **Millgarth** (GBR, 374gt/97) will be assigned. Completed at the renowned Gorinchem yard of Scheepswerf Damen on a hull built in Gdansk, twin Stork Wärtsilä engines with a combined power of over 5,000 horsepower working through two swivelling Z propellers, give a bollard pull in excess of 60 tonnes. Corporate changes in the world of ship towage mean that in her short life she has been owned by no less than three different companies, but now forms part of the Svitzer Marine group, part of the Danish Møller organisation.     (C)

There was considerable disquiet when the Corporation of Trinity House announced that it would place its order for a new lighthouse and buoy tender overseas. The order duly went to Hyundai in Korea. The decision appears to have been vindicated, for, twenty years later, the **Mermaid** (GBR, 2820gt/87) is still fully occupied around the coast servicing buoys and navigation aids. A diesel electric vessel, her four Ruston diesel generators with a combined power of 5,330 hp produce a service speed of 12 knots and the power for the deck cranes necessary to handle the many buoys that mark the navigation channels of both the Milford Haven waterway and other UK inshore waters.    (A)

For many operations in the port, the massive power and bollard pull of the harbour tugs are unnecessary and inappropriate. But tug assistance is still often required. To provide such, the Port Authority entered into a joint venture with Williams Shipping of Southampton to provide small tug services. The **Wilfreedom** (GBR, 47gt/88) is one of such vessels. Built at the Gorinchem yard of Damen Marine, the Dutch tug builders, her twin Caterpillar engines provide a bollard pull of about 11 tonnes, more than sufficient for the task of assisting the smaller tankers or coastal ships using the dry cargo and repair berths.    (B)

We have already met this ship in another guise, as the **Blackrock**. Bunkering of vessels in the port is undertaken by vessels owned by John H Whitaker and Co, a Hull-based company which has long specialised in bunkering services. In 2007, it acquired the **Blackrock**, converted her to meet the needs of the bunkering trade and renamed her **Whitdawn** (GBR, 1646gt/89). The most obvious outward signs of the conversion are the addition of the "scaling ladders" on the foredeck and the "Yokohama fenders" on the port side to enable the vessel to safely lie alongside the receiving vessel. The photograph, taken from the Coastal Path above Hazelbeach, shows her outbound from her base at the Port of Pembroke.      (E)

Milford Haven is a natural deep water port, and unlike most of its British, and indeed western European, counterparts and competitors, it has little need for costly maintenance dredging. So, the sight of a dredger actively working in the port is something of a rarity. But the expected demands and dimensions of the very large LNG ships shortly to be using the waterway have meant that it might be prudent to "shave some bottom corners". The **UKD Bluefin** (GBR, 4171gt/97) is owned by Associated British Ports Holding Ltd and operated by UK Dredging. Many of western Europe's dredgers come from Dutch shipyards, but **UKD Bluefin** is a product of the Port Glasgow yard of Ferguson Shipbuilders.      (M)

The drydock at Milford Haven is one of the few remaining operational drydocks on the west coast between Land's End and Liverpool. As such it provides a refit and repair facility for small vessels, some of which are based on or operate from the waterway. It also attracts to the port vessels which would otherwise have little or no business here. The **Amity** (GBR, 1098gt/80), one of the smallest units in the fleet of F T Everard & Co, with a deadweight tonnage of only 1,767 tonnes, was a vessel which could use the facility quite comfortably. The photo shows her being guided into the locks at Milford Docks by the small tractor tug **Neptune** which was owned and operated by the Docks Company for just such work.     (C)

Most "visitors" to the dry dock do so on a planned and regular basis for scheduled refit and repair work. Other calls are unscheduled and the customer would rather be elsewhere. The Bristol-based tug **Svitzer Brunel** (GBR, 366gt/03), one of the newer units of the Bristol tug fleet, grounded in the approaches to Portbury Docks, severely damaging her propulsion system and associated bottom plating. The incident resulted in a long unplanned stay in Milford Docks with several visits to the blocks in the dry dock to remove and repair damaged parts and to install new pieces, some of which had had to be imported from Japan.     (B)

# APPENDIX I

## NUMBERS AND GROSS TONNAGE OF SHIPPING USING THE WATERWAY

|  | 2005 | | 2006 | |
| --- | --- | --- | --- | --- |
|  | No. | TONNAGE | No. | TONNAGE |
| CHEVRON | 1,777 | 18,677,701 | 1,526 | 17,469,932 |
| SEMLOGISTICS | 195 | 3,411,026 | 120 | 1,900,294 |
| TOTAL | 691 | 6,139,608 | 616 | 6,386,356 |
| ALL REFINERY TRAFFIC | 2,663 | 28,228,335 | 2,262 | 25,756,582 |
| FERRIES | 660 | 21,850,472 | 696 | 23,135,180 |
| DRAGON LNG | 0 | 0 | 13 | 9,627 |
| SOUTH HOOK LNG | 6 | 9,093 | 28 | 47,088 |
| CROWN | 42 | 94,452 | 63 | 139,054 |
| OTHERS | 145 | 399,976 | 97 | 358,342 |
|  | 3,516 | 50,582,328 | 3,159 | 49,445,873 |

1.      Provided by the Milford Haven Port Authority, the above figures are those relating to ships paying dues.

2.      Neither LNG Terminal has yet to be completed at the time of writing. Traffic for such terminals is therefore all construction related.

3.      Information on ship tonnages can be found overleaf.

## SHIP TONNAGES

In the text, after each ship's name, we have placed certain defining details of that ship, the flag of registry, the gross tonnage, and the date of completion of the vessel. This convention enables the interested reader to trace the ship to generally accepted published records.

However, even a cursory glance will indicate that other tonnage measurements are also used in the text.

Gross tonnage (gt), a capacity measurement converting space in a vessel into an internationally agreed measurement in tonnes, is used not only in the shipping industry proper, but also by bodies such as port, river and canal authorities and governments who charge for services rendered to the ship. This internationally agreed tonnage measurement, though its definition took decades to conclude, replaced a multitude of other measurements.

Deadweight tonnage (dwt) is a measurement of the carrying capacity in tonnes of the cargo, fuel and stores which a vessel can transport. In both the oil industry and the dry bulk trades it is a commonly used standard by which ships are classified. The text of this short book follows that convention.

Naval warships, where load carrying ability is less important than seaworthiness, are generally referred to, when discussing matters of size, by the volume of water they displace, their displacement tonnage, abbreviated in the text to "displ".

## FLAG ABBREVIATIONS

| | | | |
|---|---|---|---|
| ANT | Netherlands Antilles | IOM | Isle of Man |
| ATG | Antigua & Barbuda | LBR | Liberia |
| BEL | Belgium | MHL | Marshall Islands |
| BHS | Bahamas | NIS | Norwegian International Register |
| BRB | Barbados | NLD | Netherlands |
| CYM | Cayman Islands | MLT | Malta |
| CYP | Cyprus | NOR | Norway |
| DEU | Germany | PAN | Panama |
| DIS | Danish International Register | QAT | Qatar |
| DNK | Denmark | RUS | Russia |
| ESP | Spain | SGP | Singapore |
| FRA | France | SWE | Sweden |
| GBR | United Kingdom | USA | United States of America |
| GIB | Gibraltar | VCT | St Vincent & the Grenadines |
| GRC | Greece | | |

A fine night view of the **Agility** (1930gt/90) in Milford Dock.

*(David Barrett)*

# *APPENDIX II*

## SOME THOUGHTS ON VIEWING SHIPPING ON THE WATERWAY

The Milford Haven waterway is about ten miles long.  The best viewing sites for moving marine traffic are probably on the cliff-sides on the coastal path near the villages of Angle and Dale - near Thorn Island and West Blockhouse Fort, respectively.  The area surrounding the waterway, particularly towards the west, is open countryside.  So a car, whilst not absolutely essential, is the most practical means of transport for those going ship viewing in this part of the waterway.

The Port of Pembroke is a standard UK commercial port, and there is no public access to the quayside.  However, it is a small port and views across its quays are readily available from public spaces on the seafront in the town of Pembroke Dock.

Milford Docks welcomes the public and, though areas may be restricted if a ship is alongside, the pier head and much of the dockside is routinely open to the public.  From the pier head, the view to the  south is dominated by the Chevron terminal.  For the less active or the car bound, Milford Docks pier head has much to recommend it.

The Pembrokeshire coastal path passes through the entire area, and, though this may mean a bit of energetic scrambling at times, it is possible to see and pass reasonably closely to all of the terminals.

For vessels transiting the waterway, the southern shore of the harbour offers the more practical viewing sites for the photographer, for the simple reason that the sun is behind the viewer almost all day.

The Milford Haven Port Authority website (www.mhpa.co.uk) lists both ships due and ships on berths.  But a word of warning.  The ETA listing gives Notice of Readiness times, and arrived ships may then lie off the port to await a berth, or may proceed to St Bride's Bay to anchor. Only smaller craft with Pilotage Exemption Certificates are allowed to anchor inside the harbour whilst awaiting a berth.  And there is no way of eliciting this level of information from the website data. Arrival therefore does not mean automatic entry.  The working radio channel of the Port Authority, for those with radio scanners, is Channel 12.  A listening watch on this frequency will save much fuel and frustration and will keep the swear box relatively unused.

On average, there are about 20 movements a day.  Larger loaded vessels will enter at or near to high water.  At Milford Docks, the "free flow" entry and exit takes place from two hours before high tide until the top of the tide, though "lock-ins" may take place before and after that operation.

A substantial part of the County's income comes from the tourist trade, so finding accommodation should be relatively easy, though at the height of the season, the unscheduled visitor may find the choice restricted.  The Pembrokeshire County Council operates Tourist Information Centres and can be contacted on tel. 01437 763110.  But be mindful of the fact that the small settlements of the lower waterway are just that.  So don't expect Holiday Inns, Hilton Hotels and casinos.  But the County has to its credit some very good small eating places where it is possible to eat excellent food, most of it locally produced, at metropolitan standards but at considerably better prices.

# *APPENDIX III*

## MILFORD HAVEN WATERWAY

### *Industrial sites and viewing locations*

Key to viewing locations

A  Watwick Point, Dale
B  Milford Docks
C  Milford Docks pierhead
D  The Rath, Milford Haven
E  Coast path, Semlogistics
F  Ferry Inn, Llanstadwell
G  Neyland front

H  Cleddau Bridge
J  Cosheston Pill
K  Front Street, Pembroke Dock
L  Martin's Haven
M  Coast path, Angle
N  On the waterway

Key to industrial sites

1. Milford Dock
2. Dragon LNG
3. Semlogistics
4. Waterloo Quay
5. Port of Pembroke
6. Irish Ferries
7. Carr Jetty (MoD)

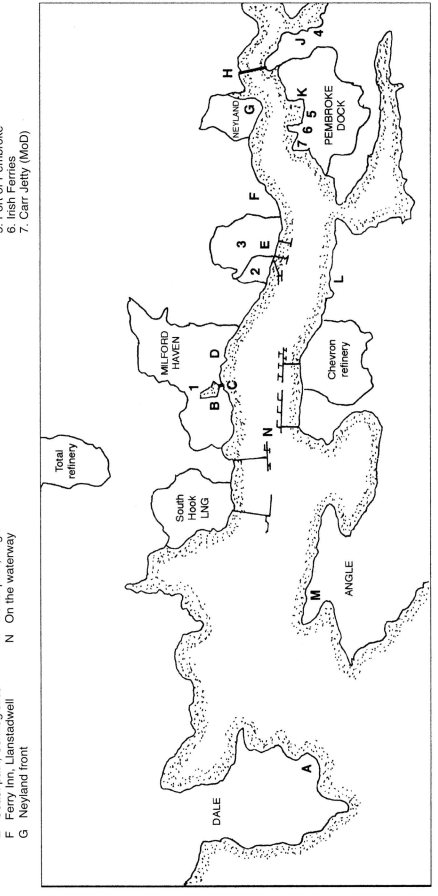

# INDEX OF SHIP NAMES